Choose a topic and start to practise writing. Each booklet has a theme to help you start to write…stories, reports, articles, letters and many more. Start collecting them now.

Guinea Pig Creative Writing booklets also provide extra practice for children who have completed:

- Creative Story Writing ISBN: 9780955831508
- Persuasive Writing & Argument ISBN: 9780955831515
- Information Writing ISBN: 9780955831522

They are for:

* children who are working at Key Stage 2 of the National Curriculum, levels 3-5 (in Years 5 and 6 of primary school),
* children who are working at Key Stage 3, levels 3-5 (Years 7 and 8 of Secondary School).

They provide practice for all 9-13 year olds, especially children taking 11+ examinations.

Written by Sally A Jones and Amanda C Jones

Published by GUINEA PIG EDUCATION

2 Cobs Way,
New Haw,
Addlestone,
Surrey,
KT15 3AF.

www.guineapigeducation.co.uk

First things first...
Let's **learn** to *write* <u>fiction</u>.

When you *write fiction*, **<u>you must</u>**:

1. Decide who will be your audience?

2. Think of different genres – realistic, detective, ghost, gothic horror.

3. Ask what is the purpose of my writing?

When you *write to entertain*, remember that **<u>you must</u>** :

1. Have an interesting opening and a memorable ending

2. Have good characters, setting and plot

3. Build up suspense

4. Use dialogue – to move the story along

5. Use a variety of simple, compound and complex sentences

Plan your fiction writing:

PARAGRAPH 1	**Write:**
• Start with a memorable first sentence to make the reader want to read on. • Introduce the characters and the setting. • Introduce the plot.	• in **FIRST PERSON**, so you are the main character telling the story (using I or we) or • in **THIRD PERSON** (using he or she) as if you were a fly watching from the wall.
PARAGRAPH 2 • Develop the plot. • What might happen to trigger off a series of events? • Build up suspense. **PARAGRAPH 3** • Wind up your story with a good ending. In the resolution you will have solved all the problems. • It could be happy, sad, a cliff hanger (which leaves the reader to make up his or her own mind), or a moral ending • Have a memorable final sentence.	**Remember:** • Use connectives or conjunctions: - *and or but (to join compound sentences)* - *or, so, if, when, while, after, before, because, unless, until, whereas, although (to join complex sentences)* - *use pronouns - who, which, whose, what, that* - *to link ideas use - firstly, later, therefore, on the other hand, at that moment, by this time, next, soon...* • Use a range of sentences – simple, compound and complex sentences

Think *about* **changes...**

On the morning the letter came, Dad had shouted out excitedly, "We're setting out on a new adventure," but I wasn't convinced I wanted to leave behind my life in the city. Two months later, removal day had come and gone, and we had arrived at our new house in the country. The hallway looked like a pigsty. It was cluttered up with piles of boxes; full of dusty old books we never read, ancient ornaments we didn't look at and other family heirlooms even Granny didn't want. There was a musty sort of smell that you associate with old things that are stored in the loft. It was a horrible muddle and looked as if we were collecting for a jumble sale. This made me feel even more miserable; the adventure hadn't got off to a good start.

"Why can't we go for a walk," I pestered Dad whose feet were hanging out of the loft. "You promised that we would explore the area."

"Look, you've got to understand," he moaned, "Mum and I have to get these crates unpacked before we start work tomorrow."

"It's just not fair," I retorted indignantly, digging my heels into the carpet. "You said you'd make time."

"We didn't know how long it would take. Look, I give you my word, that this weekend we will..." I didn't wait to hear another string of false promises from Dad, but stormed angrily down the stairs and stood contemplating the view from the big window in the lounge. There were a row of identical houses, built in the same coloured brickwork and painted in shiny white paint with a small, neat front garden laid with lawn. Suddenly, I felt isolated and alone. Something deep within me yearned to go back to the city street where I used to live. As I wrestled with my thoughts, I yearned to see again: Mr Patel's corner shop by the old railway bridge, my friend Reg and my teacher Mr Wong. My head was full of pictures of familiar places. A terrible sadness overwhelmed me. My eyes misted over. If only Dad hadn't applied for that new job.

A few minutes later I had made up my mind to go out alone. I wouldn't wait. My parents were now employed by Global Oil and started tomorrow and we had started a new life. I would explore the area myself. Swiftly I grabbed my anorak, put on my trainers and went outside, banging the door firmly behind me. I strolled purposefully down the new street. A group of boys about my own age were playing football, arguing about who scored a goal... but they ignored me completely. Had I become invisible? Was I really bothered? Deep in thought, I walked on until I came to a small park with benches and play equipment for tots. By now I was sure there was nothing here for boys like me, so I was about to turn back when I heard a voice calling me. I turned and saw a dark haired girl smiling at me through kind brown eyes. She beckoned me over.

"Are you new round here?" she asked.

"Yes, I've just moved into number 22."

"Me too, a bit further up the road. My Dad's got a new job. We've all moved to England from Dubai – me, my parents and my twin brother."

"Not Global Oil,"

"Yes, that's the one."

"My Dad works there too."

"Try a date," she added, thrusting a packet of fruit at me. "I brought them from old house. They're yummy." There was so much to talk about and I just knew we were all going to be friends. Dad was right we were going to start a new adventure.

Continue the *plan* for this story.

The opening sentences makes the reader want to read on because...

The characters are: ....

....

....

The setting is: ....

....

The plot is: having to face a big change after moving house

Introduction:

- boy's father has new job
- moved from te city to the country
- the house is full of packing boxes – is a big muddle
- boy feels miserable

Middle

- ....   Tension is when...
- ....   Suspense is...
- ....

Ending

- ....
- ....
- ....

The **ending is memorable because**..

.... and links to the beginning.

Complete the lists.

Adjective	Noun	Verb	Adverb
new	adventure	stormed	angrily
horrible	....	strolled	....
....	....	....	....

This could be the first chapter of a children's novel. The main character and his new friend could have several adventures as they explore their new life. You could write another chapter...

Now write your own story about moving to a new house. Write about how sad and lonely you felt at first, but then you met a new friend.

Write in paragraphs. Remember to start a new paragraph if you change the place, time, person or situation.

Plan your story. Think about the following points.

Write an introduction

- Have you got a good opening sentence?

- What is the setting?

- Who are the characters?

- How does he or she feel?

- How do the characters react to one another?

- What is the plot?

Middle paragraph, building up suspense

- What happens in the story?

- and after that…?

- and then…?   Build up tension and suspense.

Winding the plot up or conclusion

- How does the story end?

- Are the problems solved?

OPENING

↓

DEVELOPMENT

↓

COMPLICATION

↓

SUSPENSE & TENSION

↓

RESOLUTION

Now write the story you planned.

Let's make a journey into <u>deepest</u>, <u>darkest</u> Asia, where wild, untamed creatures live in dense, tropical jungle (rainforest)…

Let's start by developing an exciting opening sentence that gives some background information.

* Two months had passed since the fire.
* Two months had passed since that fateful day, when fire engulfed the jungle.
* Two months had passed since that fateful day, when fire engulfed the jungle and the animals had fled for their lives.

Do animals have to make changes in their lives?

Let's imagine…

Two months had passed since that fateful day, when fire engulfed the jungle and the animals had fled for their lives. Now the sun sizzled down relentlessly and the dry shrubs drooped with thirst as their roots searched the scorched ground for droplets of water. Despite the fierce heat, Stripy Tiger, Satin Puma and Little Squeak were striding purposefully along, their eyes fixed on the track in front of them. They paused only for a moment to rest.
"Not far now," Tiger reassured the others. The journey back had been so hard. His padded paws were sore with painful red blisters and the stripes on his fur were fading as the boiling saucepan of the sun burnt down on him. "We're home at last," squeaked little Squeak jumping up and down with excitement.
"Thank goodness," mumbled Puma, as they limped into the burnt clearing. It had changed.
"What has happened to our home?" they gasped. The trees had withered in the heat and the water hole had dried up. Everything was different.
"Let's find Jumbo," growled Satin Puma.
"We must see if the others got back safely," chorused the animals in unison. They trampled through the dry bush, until they came to a group of animals huddled together in despair. They were weak. They were hungry and they greeted their friends with sad grunts.
"Don't just sit there. We've got to do something to save our home," whimpered Puma.
"We must act quickly," roared Tiger.

As Tiger took control, his face lit up as his brain clicked into action. He allocated every animal with a task. He commanded the elephants to use their strength to clear away the dead logs. He made snakes slither softly over the blackened soil, smoothing out the deep cracks in the earth. Everywhere there were animals working busily: cleaning, sweeping and planting. What were they doing? They were turning the burnt up jungle back into a land bursting with colour and brightness. Now, Tiger knew he must ask for help. He stared up at the snowy white clouds. He cried out to God,
"Great one, who made the jungle and all things in it, please send us some rain to fill our water hole." Immediately, his request was answered. Out of the clouds a shower of rain trickled down. The animals, leapt, hopped and danced together. They slurped down the cool, glistening raindrops into their parched throats. The plants soaked up the life giving juice. They sighed with relief as fresh green colour filled their drooping leaves and bright radiant flowers burst into bloom. Tiger announced,
"Let's party." Every animal shrieked in delight.
"Yes, Let's party."

Try writing your own animal story.

The climate of Southeast Asia is a warm, damp climate, where huge tropical rainforests grow. Here, in countries like Malaysia and Burma, there are a huge variety of wildlife and tribes of people whose lives have remained the same for thousands of years. There is a new danger. The forest trees contain valuable timber. The logging industry is cutting down the trees and clearing the rain forest.

Imagine that you are an animal or even a tribes person living in the forest that is being cut down. Tell your story. Remember to plan your story. Make a good opening sentence.

As sunlight broke through the dense foliage, elephant paused from his drink by the waterhole. He was startled by a new sound and it was a sound he had never heard before. It was a scraping, screeching, sawing sort of sound. He remembered the warning tiger had given him before he left, 'be prepared to escape; there is trouble ahead – a danger more deadly than any predator you've ever known." What was it? It was the threat of machines coming into their home – cutting – sawing down their trees. Elephant froze with terror at the thought. MEN! MACHINES! What should he do? Should he warn the other animals?

In **paragraph 2** write:

- How the animals prepare to leave together.

- How they run to escape the men bulldozing the trees.

- Is there danger as trees fall?

- How do the characters help each other?

- Build up tension and conflict between the animals.

- How do they deal with: fear, terror? Do they run for their lives?

In **paragraph 3** write:

- Where do the animals flee to?

- Think of a place of safety where they can settle back and start a new life.

The **QUEST** to *freedom*...

1) Opening:

INTRODUCE CHARACTERS (*wild animals*), **SETTING** (*rainforest*) and the **PLOT** - a machine cutting down trees to destroy the forest. Do the animals need to escape?

2)

HUNGER

The land is cleared and the animal's food sources have gone so they are hungry.

3)

FEAR

They stampede in terror – not knowing where they will go, but with only one goal – to escape the machines.

4)

DEVELOPMENT CONFLICT

FEAR GRIPS – and he can't go on. He falls apart and weeps loudly that he will stay and die of starvation.

5)

MORE CONFLICT

One animal turns back, refusing to listen to the other animals but he is in terrible danger…

6)

TIGER TAKES CONTROL

He tells them, "be strong. We must help each other. We must believe we can overcome these dangers.

7)

The journey is hard. The conditions are bad. Food is scarce and the terrain is treacherous. The animals feet are sore.

8)

MUST STAND TOGETHER TO OVERCOME PROBLEMS

The animals choose a leader, tiger or elephant. If they are going to survive this they need to stick together. All these arguments will get them nowhere. Someone must take control and give some clear instructions.

9) Resolution:

What would be in the safe land at the end of the journey?

The animals followed the twisting river that cut a train through the dense foliage, until they came to a clearing where there was a plentiful supply of green grass, juicy shoots, green succulent leaves and a fresh spring. They drunk huge mouthfuls of fresh water and settled down to sleep in safety. They decided to make it their new home.

Now write the story you planned.

Imagine that **you** find **a box in the
attic** of your new loft. *What is in it?*

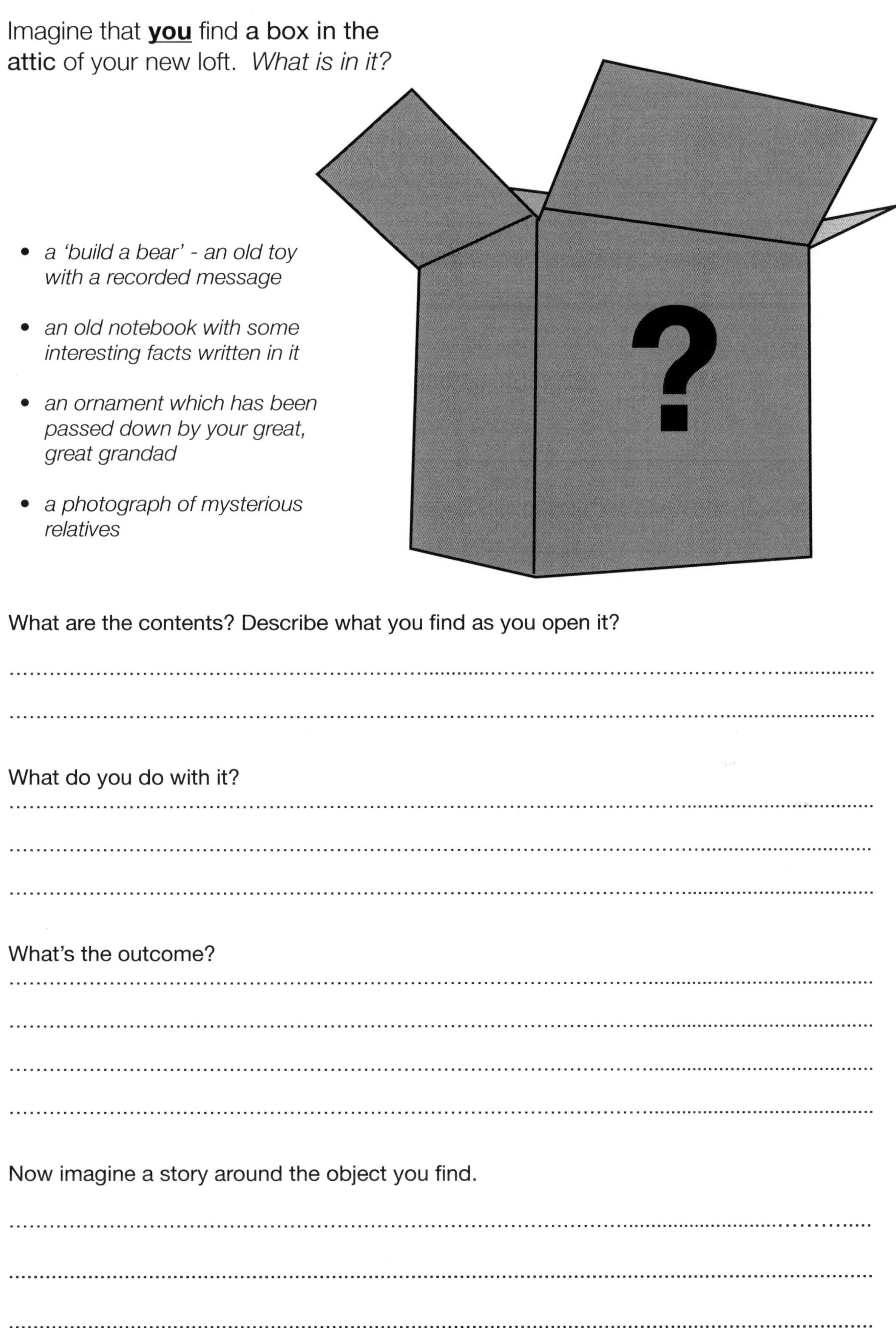

- *a 'build a bear' - an old toy
  with a recorded message*

- *an old notebook with some
  interesting facts written in it*

- *an ornament which has been
  passed down by your great,
  great grandad*

- *a photograph of mysterious
  relatives*

What are the contents? Describe what you find as you open it?

....

....

What do you do with it?

....

....

....

What's the outcome?

....

....

....

....

Now imagine a story around the object you find.

....

....

....

Think again about changes. Think about a time in your life when things changed so much, everything was different. How did you feel?

Read the diary extracts below by Sophie. She has a mum, dad, two sisters and a brother, but on moving day she was left to help her mum pack. Write your own diary about moving to another house, another school or even moving to a new country.

30th November

Friday (3 days to moving day) Help!
We're not getting on well with the packing. We started to pack, but then Grandad was taken seriously ill. How awful. We received a call from the hospital to come immediately. It had been a long night with Grandad. I remember the frantic drive up the motorway, the ghastly smell of antiseptic as we entered the door of the old people's home and seeing Grandad lying in his bed, his face as pale as marble. It made everyone sad. Of course, the packing had stopped. The clearance of the loft had come to a temporary halt. Bad news, because time was running out!

1st December

Saturday (2 days to go)
Then my big brother became ill too. Typical of him! He had volunteered to climb into the loft and sort out all the old toys, schoolbooks, rugs, curtains and all the paraphernalia you keep in there. He had thrown down boxes for the rest of the family to sort. We'd spent a lot of time reading ridiculous stories, we'd written in our textbooks when we were about eight.

We laughed and giggled until the clock struck twelve, then one, then two… But, this morning my brother became ill with flu. He couldn't find the strength to get out of bed. He felt sick and dizzy. Worse still, my two sisters also succumbed to the flu and then my Dad. Just our luck!

2nd December

Sunday Morning (One day to moving day)
"Help me," my mum screamed. "Help!" She was stressed out as usual. We have to get this lot packed in boxes. The removal men are coming at nine am tomorrow morning. "I'm doing my best," I shouted. It was manic this afternoon. Mum and I heaved all those heavy items, like an old lawn mower, a go-cart my brother had made and a pram into the car. We took them down to the storage unit, even though we'd probably never need them again. Then we queued for ages to get into the car park to buy a huge roll of bubble wrap from a DIY store. For two hours we sat together on the floor surrounded by best china. I cut off little squares of bubble wrap while mum gently covered each teacup and saucer. The clock was ticking on. My father, who looked as white as a ghost, put his head round the door to tell us he was going to the chemist. He's thought of a way of getting out of the work I thought!

Sunday Afternoon (15 hours to go)

"Work faster – even faster – Sophie, we're running out of time," gasped my frenzied mother. Suddenly, the phone rang. I was so pleased to hear a familiar voice on the other end of the line, "How are you getting on? Do you need any help?"

"Help – Yes please! Come straight round," replied my desperate mum, as she explained to Uncle John the trouble we were in.

Sunday Evening (7 hours to go)

That evening, you would have seen everyone packing industrially in our old house. It was a good sight to remember. Auntie Mona arrived, joined by Mary from next door. The former was standing on a wobbly table, passing down books to Mary to pack in boxes. After this, they used loads and loads of bubble wrap to cover my mum's prize paintings from her college days. Uncle John dismantled the wardrobes. Now we had plenty of help and the work was getting done: my dad, brother and sisters had also made some degree of recovery.

3rd December

Monday Morning

The clock chimed nine. Removal day had come, but we were in total chaos. I mean CHAOS. There were loads of half packed cardboard boxes. The removal men arrived but most of our possessions were still unpacked. Take the kitchen, for example, if you'd opened the cupboard door, you would still have seen a row of little jam pots containing my sister's home made strawberry jam.

The removal men had to radio up for reinforcements, including more men, another van and a lady from the office. They crammed all the remaining items into boxes – clothes, shoes, pots and pans and started to load them into the van. Our possessions went hurtling along the road for their new life. All that remained for us there was to collect the cat and rabbit, who were commiserating sadly with one another in their cages on the patio. We handed the keys to the new owner and left that place. To be honest – I was relieved.

Monday Afternoon

As we entered the new house, there was more disorder everywhere. There were full boxes brimming over. The removal men were battling to get the piano through the door, which was stuck at an awkward angle. Mum's favourite vase had just gone over and she was collecting up the pieces.

"How about a cuppa," sounded a jolly voice from the hall?"

"I'm desperate for one," echoed every member of the family in unison. My brother dashed out to the local Co-op and soon we were sipping tea and munching cookies. Our friend, Jennie's, face appeared around the door with two steamy casseroles of hot pasta.

"This is going to be a peaceful house," smiled Uncle John. "I just know you're going to like it here." I like Uncle John, he's so positive.

Now, write your own diary extracts about a time in your life when everything changed.

A new family, with kids your age, have moved to the street. Write a letter to welcome them.

<u>Welcome</u> to your *NEW* HOME

22 New Street,
Rushford,
Eastly,
RT34 3FG.

Dear Mrs Jones,

I would like to welcome you to your new house, because I will be your new neighbour. When I heard a new family was moving in, I was really pleased because your children are the same age as my sister and I, aged nine and eleven and I am sure we will be good friends.... *(Describe your appearance, character and interests)*

You will love living in this street because all the people are friendly, helpful and kind. We all get on well together. *(Describe the neighbours, what they are like and what they do)*

You will be pleased to know that we have good facilities in this area. There are some excellent shops, where you can buy all the things you need. The leisure centre is also close by, so you can swim or join the gym to keep fit. *(Write in more detail about local facilities, what the shops sell, about the restaurants, clubs and libraries you can join.)*

(Include a further paragraph on the local school – the teachers, timetables, uniform and special events)

I am really looking forward to meeting you. Please pop round anytime as there is always someone in. If you need any help moving, do not hesitate to knock.

Yours Sincerely,

Lucy

Decide what you want to tell your new neighbour.

Here are a few ideas.

*Note: the style is informal,
with a friendly, chatty tone.*

About us

My sister is Anastasia. She is tall, with dark hair tied back in a ponytail. She is a kind, friendly person. Her main interest is dancing: ballet, tap and modern, so she's out quite a lot of the time at lessons or practising for shows.

As for me, I'm Tanya. I'm mid height, with curly, dark hair. I prefer outdoor activities and I love to go out for a ride on my bike. Perhaps, I could show you ...

The local area

Our local neighbourhood has excellent facilities close by. At our local parade of shops, there is a library (with loads of books), a launderette and many shops including a Fresco Mini.

There are two restaurants - one is a Chinese, several churches and a mosque. There are lots of clubs you can join ... A few miles away we have a leisure centre which has... There are lots of sights only a short drive away, including ... and a river, where you can have ...

About my school

I attend ... school, but my sister goes to ... Both schools are a short distance from our house – only about a ten minutes walk, though we sometimes have to queue at the traffic lights, if we travel by car.

My school offers a wide range of subjects and gets excellent results in examinations. My favourite subject is ... because ...

All the teachers are kind, with the exception of Mr ..., who is very strict, but you'll probably only meet him if you get a detention (but I'm sure you won't). Anyway, he is a great teacher when you get to know him.

The worst thing about my school is the uniform. I wish I was a French child so I didn't have to wear one. It is ... with ... I hated it when I first went into year 7, but I'm getting used to it now.

My school is involved in ...

Now add your own ideas.

Remember to use: an introduction, points 1, 2, 3 and a conclusion.

Now write your letter.

Your cousins are about to go to big school. Write a letter advising them what it will be like changing to big school and the problems they might encounter.   You will find some ideas on the next page.

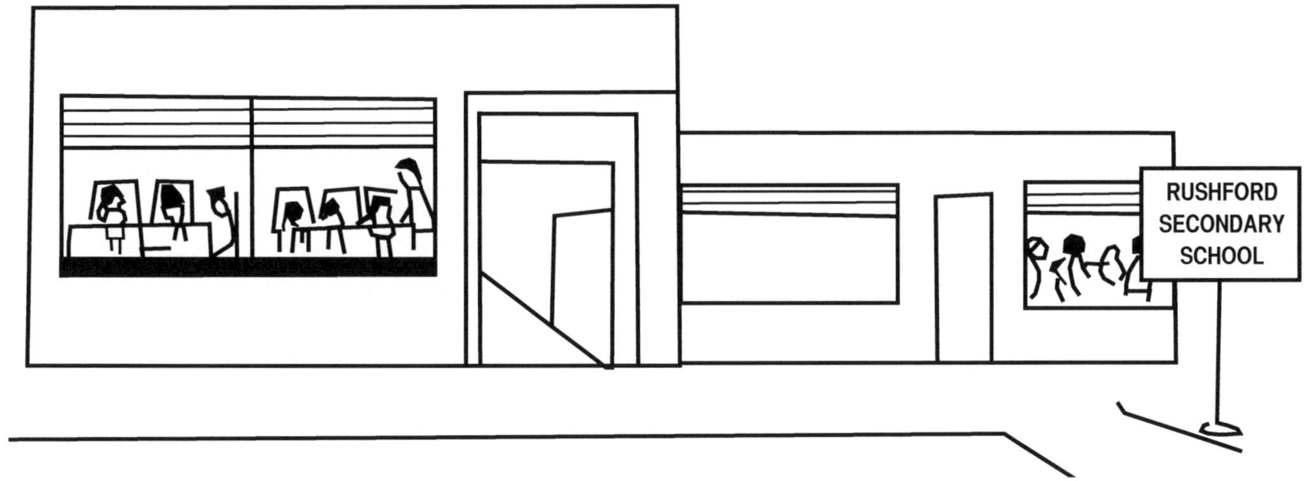

To **advise** someone, is to *help them understand* or cope with something.

- Point out the difficulties and the benefits. Explain what problems they might have and suggest solutions to those problems.

- Use a kind tone. (Year sevens might be nervous at first)

- Make some anecdote – personal stories told in a few lines.
  'When I was at school I got bullied because...'

- Address your reader directly.

<u>Vocabulary</u>

- You might consider...
- It would be best if...
- I think you might like...
- Don't worry if you...
- It's going to be...

Here are changes you might experience moving from primary to big (secondary) school. Can you think of any more? Use these notes to write your letter. Select the points you want to use and then write them up in paragraphs.

Points I want to make:

- Big school will be great. Don't panic. You'll soon get used to it.

- Remember, all these people were new kids at some time.

- Be confident and know that you're older now and will soon be able to cope with the long walk around school, the horrendous timetable with different subjects – like chemistry and physics and all that homework!

- Don't get stressed. Keep calm. Take the opportunity to befriend new people who have been to different schools and have had slightly different experiences.

- If you don't get on well with someone, there are plenty of other people to befriend.

- Get a suitable lightweight rucksack, with compartments to organise your work into different subjects.

- You'll soon get used to the routine. Organise your school things so you bring only the things you require every day.

- Your new friends will help you to find your way around.

- Your tutor will also help you if anyone is mean to you or bullies you.

- Always ask for help if you need it.

- Respect the school rules. For example, always wear your school uniform.

- After a few weeks, you will feel like you have been at big school for years.

- It will take time to get used to the changes.

- You've been used to primary school where you had:
    - one teacher
    - the same class room, where you remained for most of the day
    - a small class of only 20 children.

- Big school will seem busy. There will be crowds of people of all ages.

- You will have to get to know your way round a huge school, with endless corridors that look the same, when you move to each lesson.

- You will have to get to know where your classrooms are.

- You will have lots of different teachers to help and support you with your work.

- You will have a lot of heavy books to carry round.

- You will be able to join some extra curriculum activities. You can read the school notice board for information on school clubs.

- Your school will give you a homework planner or timetable.

- Your form tutor will be there to help you with any problems.

- Students achieve high levels at this school, because:
    - they work hard
    - the teachers are helpful
    - there are classroom buddies.

Plan your letter. Use the notes on the following pages.

83 Gilmore Cresecent,

Rushford,

RG45 3DF

Date

Dear ....,

I understand how difficult it can be starting secondary school.
Therefore, I thought I'd write to you to set your mind at ease and let you
know what you can expect on your first day.

Point 1: ....
....
....
....

Point 2: ....
....
....
....

Point 3: ....
....
....
....

Point 4: ....
....
....

Conclusion: ....
....
....

Now write your letter.

Made in the USA
Monee, IL
07 July 2026

56552020R00017